the best
of me

We create our books with love and great care.

Yet mistakes can always happen. For any issues with your journal, such as faulty binding, printing errors, or something else, please do not hesitate to contact us at: **hello@happinesscreators.com**. We will make sure you get a replacement copy immediately.

For any suggestions or questions regarding our books, please contact us at: **hello@happinesscreators.com**

ISBN: 978-8412487411

Without your voice we don't exist.
Please, support us and leave a review!

Thank you!

You deserve to be happy, healthy and loved.

This journal has one goal:

to help you to get in your best shape physically, mentally and spiritually, and learn in the process to love and accept yourself.

HOW TO USE THIS JOURNAL

(a few words about the sections we have chosen to include on each page and why)

GRATITUDE:

We cannot stress enough how important and beneficial it is to cultivate an attitude of gratitude. Numerous scientific studies show that people who regularly take time to notice things they are grateful for enjoy better sleep, better relationships, greater resolve towards achieving goals, reduce their stress and lifetime risk for depression, show more compassion and kindness, and are overall happier.

By beginning the day with gratitude, we train our minds to look for the positive rather than focusing on the challenges and frustrations we have encountered throughout the week.

Gratitude doesn't have to be only about the big things. You can be thankful for a nice cup of coffee, a sunny winter day, or that adorable silly butt-wiggle dance your dog makes when you come home.

A simple routine but probably most beneficial for your happiness.

DAILY GOALS:

Setting your daily goals will make it more likely to follow through on them. Narrow your list to a small, manageable number to have time, energy and motivation to focus on your goals mindfully and thoroughly, and enjoy the satisfaction when you complete them.

MOOD:

Being mindful of your emotions can help identify the true reasons for your lifestyle choices and eating habits, and what triggers them.

DRINKING WATER:

There are so many scientifically proven health benefits to drinking water: water flushes out toxins, helps keep your joints lubricated and flexible, boosts metabolism, improves skin complexion, regulates body temperature, maintains blood pressure, powers your workouts, suppresses appetite and can promote weight loss.

Our advice: Start each day with a glass of water. It will fire up your metabolism and increase your mental and physical performance during the day.

SLEEP:

Sleep is vital for maintaining good mental and physical health. A good night's sleep can help boost your immune system, improve your learning, memory, concentration, decision-making, and even your creativity.

FOOD:

What you eat matters, whether you want to lose weight, be healthy or just want to be happy. And for each of these goals keeping a food diary is very beneficial.

Food diaries allow dieticians and other health professionals to recognize how your food choices impact your health.

But did you know that keeping a food journal is considered #1 key strategy for weight loss? Studies show that people who keep daily food journals lose twice as much weight compared to those without food journals.

And did you know that what you eat affects your mood? Food can promote or reduce our mental well-being.

Having said all of the above, it is clear why food journals are a valued tool recognized by dietitians, health coaches and therapists.

EXERCISE:

Physical activity improves memory and brain function, overall health, your quality of sleep, mood, confidence, boosts energy, and aids in weight management.

Get moving even if it is for small bits of time here and there. And record your physical activity and workouts because this will help you stay consistent and motivated.

REFLECTION PAGES

We have left a dedicated page after each 7 days where you can track your progress, reflect on how the week has gone by and see what you can improve so that each following week will go better than the previous one.

You can skip the reflection pages whenever you like or leave them for later. You can fill in only a certain section (and that applies to all pages of the journal), that is up to you.

Just be consistent and try to write in your journal every day because this will help you achieve the best results.

* * *

By all means, this journal is not created to tell you how to live your life. It cannot miraculously make all your personal problems and insecurities disappear. But every single page of it is created with so much love and the sole intention to help you to

get in your best shape physically, mentally and spiritually, and learn to love and accept yourself.

Know that this cannot happen without your determination and efforts, and acknowledge and appreciate your own courage that is needed to start this journey.

And finally, even with all our good intentions, our journal is not a substitute for medical or other professional advice. There is nothing shameful in needing help for your mental or physical health. If you are in this position, please, seek professional help for yourself.

week 1	1	2	3	4	5	6	7
week 2	8	9	10	11	12	13	14
week 3	15	16	17	18	19	20	21
week 4	22	23	24	25	26	27	28
week 5	29	30	31	32	33	34	35
week 6	36	37	38	39	40	41	42
week 7	43	44	45	46	47	48	49
week 8	50	51	52	53	54	55	56
week 9	57	58	59	60	61	62	63
week 10	64	65	66	67	68	69	70
week 11	71	72	73	74	75	76	77
week 12	78	79	80	81	82	83	84
week 13	85	86	87	88	89	90	91
week 14	92	93	94	95	96	97	98
week 15	99	100					

30 Days
to start forming
NEW HABITS

Track your food ... or don't.
Track your weight ... or don't.
Track your habits ... or don't.
But do have an
ATTITUDE of
GRATITUDE.

Cross a BIG X
over each day you are
PROUD
of your efforts

60 Days
to enjoy a
CHANGING YOU

Time to
CELEBRATE
your progress

100 Days
to transform your
BODY & MIND

My Thoughts

Be
the best
of You!

DAY 1

___/___/___

How I feel today:

○ ☹ ○ 😐 ○ ☺

START WITH GRATITUDE

Today I am grateful about...

PRIORITY GOALS

ONE DAY OR DAY ONE.
YOU DECIDE.

BREAKFAST

LUNCH

WATER

DINNER

SNACKS

SLEEP TIME

List 3 things you would like to IMPROVE *about yourself*

EXERCISE / ACTIVITY

DAY 2

___/___/___

How I feel today:

○ ☹ ○ 😐 ○ ☺

START WITH GRATITUDE

Today I am grateful about...

PRIORITY GOALS

You can, you should, and if you are brave enough to start, you will.

– STEPHEN KING

WATER

BREAKFAST

LUNCH

SLEEP TIME

DINNER

SNACKS

How many times have you felt fear and discouragement just by thinking about how far your goal is and how much effort you need to put to get there?

Focus on today. Force yourself to be brave and face the challenges one day at a time.

You will get there!

EXERCISE / ACTIVITY

DAY 3

___/___/___

How I feel today:

○ ☹ ○ 😐 ○ ☺

START WITH GRATITUDE

Today I am grateful about...

PRIORITY GOALS

Your body hears everything your mind says. Stay positive.

BREAKFAST

LUNCH

WATER

DINNER

SNACKS

SLEEP TIME

List 3 things (or more) YOU LIKE *about yourself*

EXERCISE / ACTIVITY

DAY 4

__/__/__

How I feel today:

START WITH GRATITUDE

Today I am grateful about...

PRIORITY GOALS

Feeling down? Did you know that our bodies might respond to negative emotions with headaches, back pain, upset stomach, increased inflammation, unwanted weight gain or loss, to name a few? You may have the "perfect" diet and exercise plan and still not achieve positive results if your thoughts remain negative.

That doesn't mean you need to deny your negative feelings. Acknowledge them but focus on something good. Direct your thoughts to something positive.

BREAKFAST

LUNCH

WATER

SLEEP TIME

DINNER

SNACKS

EXERCISE / ACTIVITY

think Happy thoughts

DAY 5

___/___/___

How I feel today:

○ ☹ ○ 😐 ○ ☺

START WITH GRATITUDE

Today I am grateful about...

PRIORITY GOALS

Every new day is another chance to change your life.

BREAKFAST

LUNCH

WATER

DINNER

SNACKS

SLEEP TIME

What makes you
HAPPY?
How can you do more of it?

EXERCISE / ACTIVITY

DAY 6

___/___/___

How I feel today:

○ ☹ ○ 😐 ○ ☺

START WITH GRATITUDE

Today I am grateful about...

PRIORITY GOALS

Just believe in yourself. Even if you don't, pretend that you do and someday you will.

– VENUS WILLIAMS

BREAKFAST

LUNCH

DINNER

SNACKS

WATER

SLEEP TIME

EXERCISE / ACTIVITY

What is your positive AFFIRMATION *for today?*

DAY 7

___/___/___

How I feel today:

○ ☹ ○ 😐 ○ ☺

START WITH GRATITUDE

Today I am grateful about...

PRIORITY GOALS

Dream big. Start small. But most of all, start.

Often times we don't take action because we believe that we have to make all the necessary changes at once and we are simply not ready for that.

Begin with small steps. Drink an extra cup of water today. Add a few green leaves to your meal tomorrow. Do 7 minutes of exercise the next day. Small steps in the right direction is always better than no action at all.

BREAKFAST

LUNCH

WATER

DINNER

SNACKS

SLEEP TIME

EXERCISE / ACTIVITY

Let yourself
DREAM A LITTLE.
Close your eyes and imagine
YOUR BEST
POSSIBLE SELF.
Imagine the person you want to become, how you will feel, think and behave, how others will know you are at your best.

THIS WEEK'S REFLECTION

THE POWER OF SMALL BUT CONSISTENT STEPS

Don't give up when your big plans and bold ambitions to change your life don't happen overnight, or even in a few days or weeks. Your best chance of getting great results is to stop pushing for large, dramatic changes. Instead, focus on the teeny tiny steps that you can be consistent about.

Long-term consistency beats short-term intensity.

– BRUCE LEE

arm [1] ....

chest [2] ....

waist [3] ....

hips [4] ....

thigh [5] ....

calf [6] ....

weight ....

This powerful principle can be applied to any aspect in life, whether trying to lose weight, start a career, or maintain a romantic relationship. Or to put it in simple examples:

» Small everyday kind words and actions are better than grand one-time romantic gestures.

» Doing a little yoga often is better than doing a lot but rarely.

THINGS TO IMPROVE:

THINK OF 3 GOOD THINGS THAT HAPPENED THIS WEEK:

DAY 8

___/___/___

How I feel today:

○ ☹ ○ 😐 ○ ☺

START WITH GRATITUDE

Today I am grateful about...

PRIORITY GOALS

The past cannot be changed. The future is yet in your power.

Yesterday is what it is. Tomorrow is just a decision away. Decide to work on creating a better and happier future for yourself.

BREAKFAST

LUNCH

DINNER

SNACKS

WATER

SLEEP TIME

To keep your spirits up set 3 simple, easy-to-complete, GOALS FOR THIS WEEK.

EXERCISE / ACTIVITY

DAY 9

/ /

How I feel today:

START WITH GRATITUDE

Today I am grateful about...

PRIORITY GOALS

Happiness is not a big thing.
It is a million little things.

BREAKFAST

LUNCH

DINNER

SNACKS

WATER

SLEEP TIME

EXERCISE / ACTIVITY

What things or
MOMENTS FROM TODAY
would you like to do
or have again tomorrow?

DAY 10

___/___/___

How I feel today:

○ ☹ ○ 😐 ○ 🙂

START WITH GRATITUDE

Today I am grateful about...

PRIORITY GOALS

You are the average of the five people you spend the most time with.

– JIM ROHN

WATER

BREAKFAST

LUNCH

SLEEP TIME

You are who you hang out with,

so choose your friends wisely and carefully.

Surround yourself with people who are positive, kind, supportive and don't make you question your worth. Spend time with those who make you feel happy and fulfilled.

This will increase your own positivity and happiness levels.

DINNER

SNACKS

EXERCISE / ACTIVITY

DAY 11

___/___/___

How I feel today:

○ ☹ ○ 😐 ○ ☺

START WITH GRATITUDE

Today I am grateful about...

PRIORITY GOALS

We often focus on how to be independent, be enough for ourselves, achieve anything on our own.

Today, honor those who have been there for you, who have helped you during a rough time, or who have inspired you.

WATER

SLEEP TIME

BREAKFAST

LUNCH

DINNER

SNACKS

EXERCISE / ACTIVITY

Love and THANKS

Say
THANK YOU
to these people:

DAY 12

/ /

How I feel today:

START WITH GRATITUDE

Today I am grateful about...

PRIORITY GOALS

It is a long process but quitting will not speed it up.

WATER

BREAKFAST

LUNCH

SLEEP TIME

DINNER

SNACKS

Stay committed and focused.

No one said that becoming the best version of yourself was easy, fast and free of setbacks. But

there is only one sure way to fail: giving up.

EXERCISE / ACTIVITY

DAY 13

__/__/__

How I feel today:

○ ☹ ○ 😐 ○ ☺

START WITH GRATITUDE

Today I am grateful about...

PRIORITY GOALS

Mistakes are the proof that you are trying.

– JENNIFER LIM

So, you slipped. Big deal!

Your past mistakes cannot be undone, and neither there is guarantee you will avoid them in future. Learn from your mistakes, adapt, change your approach, try again, repeat.

BREAKFAST

LUNCH

WATER

DINNER

SNACKS

SLEEP TIME

What, if anything, went wrong today and how can you

DO BETTER TOMORROW?

EXERCISE / ACTIVITY

DAY 14

___/___/___

How I feel today:

○ ☹ ○ 😐 ○ ☺

START WITH GRATITUDE

Today I am grateful about...

PRIORITY GOALS

In solitude the mind gains strength and learns to lean upon itself.

– LAURENCE STERNE

BREAKFAST

LUNCH

WATER

SLEEP TIME

DINNER

SNACKS

Take a step back from all the noise and chaos of the world that surrounds you. Spend

10 "think minutes"

alone, away from other people or technology.

EXERCISE / ACTIVITY

Staying alone with your thoughts

from time to time is essential for your mental health and personal growth. It gives you a chance to learn more about yourself and often times find the answers to your questions.

THIS WEEK'S REFLECTION

WHAT ARE YOUR SUPERPOWERS?

Most of us easily identify our weaknesses, but struggle to name our natural strengths and talents. Not only that, but when we think of improving ourselves, we normally think of a weakness that we have, not a strength.

But research shows that people who recognize and use their strengths are generally more successful. We experience faster growth if we focus on developing our strengths rather than trying to eliminate our weaknesses.

If at this point you think, "I am not really excelling at anything", stop! Everybody has their own strengths. Work on developing them and turn them into your superpowers.

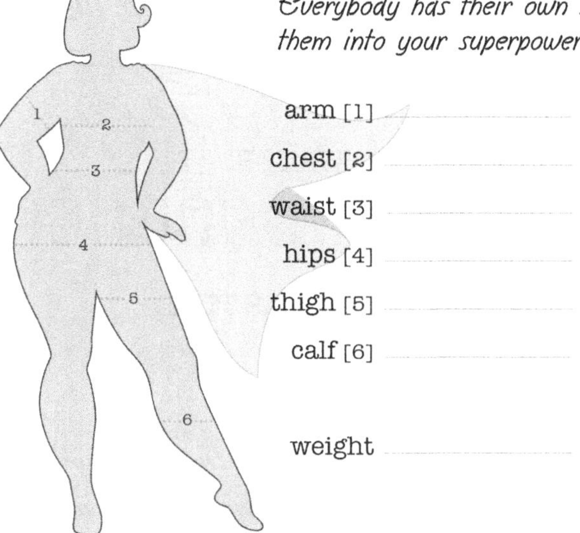

Are you persistent? Resourceful? Creative? Compassionate? Funny? Kind? A good friend? A good listener? A good motivator? A good dancer?

Finish the sentence: ***I am...***

THINGS TO IMPROVE:

THINK OF 3 GOOD THINGS THAT HAPPENED THIS WEEK:

DAY 15

___/___/___

How I feel today:

○ ☹ ○ 😐 ○ ☺

START WITH GRATITUDE

Today I am grateful about...

PRIORITY GOALS

Our bodies change our minds,
and our minds can change our behavior.

BREAKFAST

LUNCH

WATER

SLEEP TIME

DINNER

SNACKS

This week focus on tricking your brain into feelings of HAPPINESS & CONFIDENCE.

EXERCISE / ACTIVITY

Google
Amy Cuddy 2012 TED talk
and watch it.

DAY 16

___/___/___

How I feel today:

○ ☹ ○ 😐 ○ ☺

START WITH GRATITUDE

Today I am grateful about...

PRIORITY GOALS

and our behavior can change our outcomes.

– AMY CUDDY

BREAKFAST

LUNCH

WATER

SLEEP TIME

DINNER

SNACKS

EXERCISE / ACTIVITY

Did you know that standing in a posture of confidence, even if you don't feel confident, can actually boost your confidence?

Try this simple powerful trick:

next time before a stressful event (like a job interview, an important meeting, etc.) spend 2 minutes in a "power pose" (think Superman or Wonder Woman). This simple act will change your hormones and the way you ultimately feel and perform.

DAY 17

__/__/__

How I feel today:

○  ○  ○ 

START WITH GRATITUDE

Today I am grateful about...

PRIORITY GOALS

Tiny tweaks can lead to big changes.

– AMY CUDDY

BREAKFAST

LUNCH

WATER

DINNER

SNACKS

SLEEP TIME

EXERCISE / ACTIVITY

If you have negative thoughts

don't slump over or bend your head. This will only validate them and make you feel worse. Instead, write those thoughts down on a piece of paper, and then throw it away in the trash. This symbolic act will make you less affected by your negative thoughts.

Try it!

DAY 18

/ /

How I feel today:

○ ☹ ○ 😐 ○ ☺

START WITH GRATITUDE

Today I am grateful about...

PRIORITY GOALS

Try this smile challenge: ***Smile at yourself in the mirror*** *first thing in the morning for at least a week.*

It might feel silly at first but smiling has many benefits for your well-being. Smiling slows the heart and relaxes the body, releases endorphins and diminishes stress hormones, increases productivity, and strengthens the immune system.

Smiling, as it turns out, prompts your brain to produce feel-good hormones and activates your brain's happiness circuitry. As a result, smiling makes you feel good regardless of your current mood in the moment. So go ahead and

Just smile

BREAKFAST

LUNCH

DINNER

SNACKS

EXERCISE / ACTIVITY

WATER

SLEEP TIME

DAY 19

__/__/__

How I feel today:

START WITH GRATITUDE

Today I am grateful about...

PRIORITY GOALS

Serotonin: The Natural Mood Booster

Serotonin is the hormone responsible for boosting mood. Low levels of serotonin are linked to depression.

BREAKFAST

LUNCH

DINNER

SNACKS

EXERCISE / ACTIVITY

Simply standing up straight (shoulders back, chin down, chest up) will result in increased levels of serotonin being released in the brain.

Stand up straight.

WATER

SLEEP TIME

DAY 20

___/___/___

START WITH GRATITUDE

Today I am grateful about...

How I feel today:

○ ☹ ○ 😐 ○ ☺

PRIORITY GOALS

Dopamine: The Pathway to Motivation and Pleasure

Dopamine in large amounts creates feelings of pleasure and reward. Low levels lead to reduced motivation and enthusiasm. There is also a strong link between dopamine dysfunction and obesity.

BREAKFAST

LUNCH

DINNER

SNACKS

EXERCISE / ACTIVITY

So how to increase dopamine naturally?

Exercise.

Whenever you exercise your brain releases dopamine.

But you can also get a surge of dopamine from things like listening to music, meditating, eating protein-rich foods, and achieving a goal, large or small.

WATER

SLEEP TIME

DAY 21

___/___/___

How I feel today:

○ ☹ ○ 😐 ○ ☺

START WITH GRATITUDE

Today I am grateful about...

PRIORITY GOALS

The Power of a Simple Hug as a Natural Anti-Depressant

Scientists found that during 20 seconds of continuous hugging we release oxytocin, a hormone that relaxes us and lowers anxiety.
Just the simple act of touch also seems to boost oxytocin release. Giving someone a massage, cuddling, making love, or giving someone a hug leads to higher levels of this hormone and a greater sense of well-being.

BREAKFAST

LUNCH

WATER

SLEEP TIME

DINNER

SNACKS

Who are the people that mean the most to you?
GIVE THEM A HUG
and tell them you love them.

EXERCISE / ACTIVITY

THIS WEEK'S REFLECTION

In summary:

DON'T FORGET TO GET YOUR DAILY DOSE OF HAPPINESS.

Boost your happiness by boosting the four feel-good hormones known as DOSE*:*

Dopamine, Oxytocin, Serotonin, and Endorphins.

These chemicals can be naturally boosted through proper diet, exercise, exposure to sunshine, and activities that you enjoy, such as dancing.

Oxytocin
(give a hug)

Serotonin
(stand up straight)

Endorphins
(smile)

Dopamine
(get moving)

1
2
3
4
5
6

arm [1] ....

chest [2] ....

waist [3] ....

hips [4] ....

thigh [5] ....

calf [6] ....

weight ....

AFFIRMATIONS

I am...

THINGS TO IMPROVE:

THINK OF 3 GOOD THINGS THAT HAPPENED THIS WEEK:

DAY 22

___/___/___

How I feel today:

○ ☹ ○ 😐 ○ ☺

START WITH GRATITUDE

Today I am grateful about...

PRIORITY GOALS

The mind is everything.
What you think you become.

BREAKFAST

LUNCH

WATER

SLEEP TIME

Dedicate
5 minutes today
to think about
how you want to see
yourself in 5 years.
Imagine how you will feel then. Write it down and look at it at least once a day this week.

DINNER

SNACKS

EXERCISE / ACTIVITY

DAY 23

___/___/___

How I feel today:

○  ○  ○ 

START WITH GRATITUDE

Today I am grateful about...

PRIORITY GOALS

To succeed you need to find something to hold on to, something to motivate you, something to inspire you.

– TONY DORSETT

BREAKFAST

LUNCH

People who are generally more inspired in their daily lives tend to set inspired goals. Goals that inspire us are more likely to be successfully attained.

DINNER

SNACKS

WATER

SLEEP TIME

EXERCISE / ACTIVITY

List 3 people who

INSPIRE YOU

DAY 24

___/___/___

How I feel today:

○  ○  ○ 

START WITH GRATITUDE

Today I am grateful about...

PRIORITY GOALS

Water is the driving force of all nature.

– LEONARDO DA VINCI

WATER

SLEEP TIME

BREAKFAST

LUNCH

We are made of water. Every single cell of our body needs water.
Very often when we feel tired, lethargic, or have a headache, it is because we are dehydrated. Don't forget to

drink a lot of water.

DINNER

SNACKS

EXERCISE / ACTIVITY

Drink a glass of
WATER
when you wake up –
a simple and easy way to
BOOST YOUR
METABOLISM

DAY 25

/ /

How I feel today:

○ ☹ ○ 😐 ○ ☺

START WITH GRATITUDE

Today I am grateful about...

PRIORITY GOALS

Happiness consists in getting enough sleep. Just that, nothing more.

– ROBERT A. HEINLEIN

WATER

BREAKFAST

LUNCH

SLEEP TIME

Getting a good night's sleep is just as important for your health as eating well and exercising.

Numerous studies have associated sleeping fewer than 7 hours per night with a greater risk of weight gain.

To make matters worse, to compensate for lack of energy, sleep deprivation may make you crave foods that are higher in sugar and fat because of their higher calorie content.

So tonight

get enough sleep!

DINNER

SNACKS

EXERCISE / ACTIVITY

DAY 26

___/___/___

How I feel today:

START WITH GRATITUDE

Today I am grateful about...

PRIORITY GOALS

Music heals the soul.

BREAKFAST

LUNCH

WATER

SLEEP TIME

DINNER

SNACKS

Music is recognized as an evidence-based form of therapy; it can lower your blood pressure, help you manage pain, help alleviate the symptoms of depression, anxiety, and other mood disorders, and increase motivation.

Make some time to listen to your FAVORITE SONGS TODAY. *What are they?*

EXERCISE / ACTIVITY

DAY 27

How I feel today:

START WITH GRATITUDE

Today I am grateful about...

PRIORITY GOALS

Dear stomach, you are bored, not hungry. So, shut up!

BREAKFAST

LUNCH

WATER

SLEEP TIME

DINNER

SNACKS

EXERCISE / ACTIVITY

Are you eating out of boredom? One reason is dopamine. When we are bored, our brains are not stimulated and dopamine levels drop. Food craving is one of the tools our brain uses to bring them back up.

Find an enjoyable activity or
HOBBY THAT INVOLVES YOUR HANDS.

It is a win-win on many levels. When you keep your hands busy you can do only one activity at a time. In the same time, doing something you enjoy will reduce negative stress, and as your skills grow, increase your confidence and self-esteem.

DAY 28

___/___/___

How I feel today:

START WITH GRATITUDE

Today I am grateful about...

PRIORITY GOALS

In two weeks, you will feel it.
In four weeks, you will see it.
In eight weeks, you will hear it.

BREAKFAST

LUNCH

WATER

SLEEP TIME

DINNER

SNACKS

EXERCISE / ACTIVITY

THIS WEEK'S REFLECTION

DO YOU EVER SAY THANK YOU TO YOURSELF?

If you are thinking "I didn't do enough" or "I didn't exercise" or "I didn't eat healthy" or "I keep making the same mistakes", it may be a sign that you don't appreciate yourself enough.

Thank yourself for the efforts. Thank yourself for trying to be better, to learn and grow. Or thank yourself for the awareness of what you need to change.

If you make a conscious effort to appreciate all the things you do, no matter how small, you will learn to truly love and appreciate yourself.

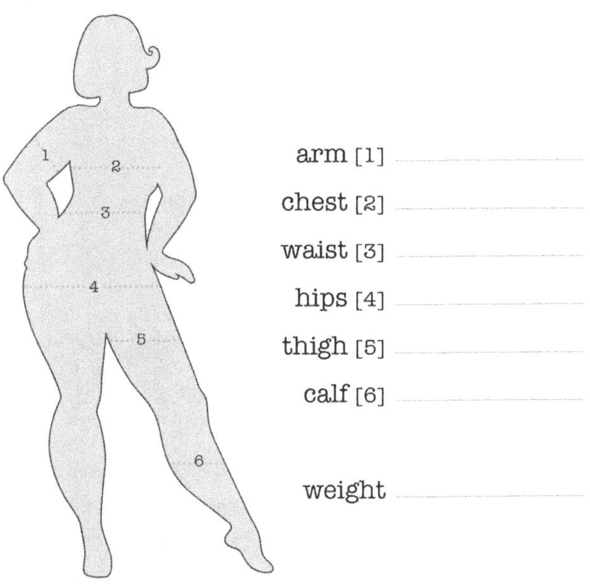

arm [1] ....

chest [2] ....

waist [3] ....

hips [4] ....

thigh [5] ....

calf [6] ....

weight ....

THINGS TO IMPROVE:

THINK OF 3 GOOD THINGS THAT HAPPENED THIS WEEK:

DAY 29

___/___/___

How I feel today:

○ ☹ ○ 😐 ○ ☺

START WITH GRATITUDE

Today I am grateful about...

PRIORITY GOALS

Wake up with determination.

What are you going to accomplish today to make progress towards achieving your goals?

WATER

BREAKFAST

LUNCH

SLEEP TIME

DINNER

SNACKS

EXERCISE / ACTIVITY

This week, every time you wake up in the morning try to set one

SMALLER, ACHIEVABLE GOAL

for the day.

It doesn't have to be something that you will repeat every day but do try to choose something that will bring you closer to your objective. For example, "today I will finally drink 8 glasses of water", or "the entire day today I will pick the stairs over the elevator", etc. This will help you start your day off with the right mindset and end it with satisfaction.

DAY 30

___/___/___

How I feel today:

○ ☹ ○ 😐 ○ ☺

START WITH GRATITUDE

Today I am grateful about...

PRIORITY GOALS

Go to bed with satisfaction.

End your day feeling good.

WATER

SLEEP TIME

BREAKFAST

LUNCH

DINNER

SNACKS

This week try to

GO TO BED ALWAYS WITH A POSITIVE THOUGHT.

Focus on one positive thing that happened today or one positive thing of tomorrow you are excited about.

EXERCISE / ACTIVITY

What went great today?

DAY 31

/ /

How I feel today:

START WITH GRATITUDE

Today I am grateful about...

PRIORITY GOALS

Seek inspiration.

It is hard to feel good and motivated for a considerable length of time. A simple solution to stay on track with your goals is to inspire yourself each day.

BREAKFAST

LUNCH

WATER

SLEEP TIME

DINNER

SNACKS

EXERCISE / ACTIVITY

Every day try to dedicate a few minutes to

WATCH MOTIVATIONAL VIDEOS

on YouTube, or through TED Talks, or other means. Let others' life stories inspire and empower you.

DAY 32

__ / __ / __

How I feel today:

○ ☹ ○ 😐 ○ ☺

START WITH GRATITUDE

Today I am grateful about...

PRIORITY GOALS

Schedule the time for what makes you happy.

You probably won't enjoy taking time for yourself if you know there is something else you need to be doing. So schedule the time for the little things that make you feel good. Watch an episode of your favorite TV show, listen to your favorite music, take a bath, etc.

BREAKFAST

LUNCH

WATER

SLEEP TIME

DINNER

SNACKS

Doing more of what makes you happy is not a luxury, it is

essential for your well-being!

EXERCISE / ACTIVITY

What is one
MOVIE OR TV SHOW
that always makes you happy?

DAY 33

___/___/___

How I feel today:

○ ☹ ○ 😐 ○ ☺

START WITH GRATITUDE

Today I am grateful about...

PRIORITY GOALS

A good life is a collection of happy memories.

– DENIS WAITLEY

WATER

BREAKFAST

LUNCH

SLEEP TIME

happy memories

Studies show that remembering happier times can be an effective protection against stress and depression. It can fuel feelings of gratitude and help you get rid of negative thoughts.

DINNER

SNACKS

What POSITIVE MEMORY *makes you happy?*

EXERCISE / ACTIVITY

DAY 34

___/___/___

How I feel today:

○  ○  ○ 

START WITH GRATITUDE

Today I am grateful about...

PRIORITY GOALS

Rule One is never quit. Rule Two is refer to Rule One. Cake happens, but as long as you remember those rules, you'll be OK.

– JAIMIE, WW LEADER

BREAKFAST

LUNCH

WATER

SLEEP TIME

DINNER

SNACKS

EXERCISE / ACTIVITY

If you are going to eat that cake (or chocolate, or ice-cream, etc), stop everything else and do only that. Don't look at your phone at the same time. Don't watch TV. Focus only on the pleasurable sensations it will give you.

How does it taste? How does it smell? How is your body reacting to what you are eating?

Forget the guilty feelings. You deserve happy moments even if they come from food from time to time.

Just be mindful of every second of it and truly enjoy every bite.

DAY 35

___/___/___

How I feel today:

○ ☹ ○ 😐 ○ ☺

START WITH GRATITUDE

Today I am grateful about...

PRIORITY GOALS

When you stop worrying about what you cannot control, you have time to change the things you can control, and that changes everything.

BREAKFAST

LUNCH

WATER

SLEEP TIME

Whenever you worry, ask yourself, "Is this a problem I can solve?"

If it's within your control,

tackle the problem.

For example, if you want to get in better shape, do your best to eat healthy and exercise.

If it's out of your control,

change your emotional state and practice acceptance.

For example, if you want targeted fat loss, know that you cannot control where on your body you lose weight from. Healthy, fit bodies come in all shapes and sizes. Learn to love the body you've been given and then take steps to make it as healthy and strong as you can.

DINNER

SNACKS

EXERCISE / ACTIVITY

THIS WEEK'S REFLECTION

THE POWER OF POSITIVE THINKING

Noticing the good things in your life is a skill that can be improved and developed. Even if you are not a naturally optimistic person, daily practice can make it easier over time.

At first it may seem a hard task but don't get discouraged.

At the end of each day consciously try to rewind in your mind the events of that day and look for one little good thing. And then another one. And another one.

The more you focus on the positives, the more you'll notice them in your life.

Like your favorite song playing randomly on the radio. Or the smell outside after the rain has stopped. Or climbing into bed when you have fresh sheets. Or a compliment from a colleague that you normally wouldn't notice or even believe.

arm [1] ________

chest [2] ________

waist [3] ________

hips [4] ________

thigh [5] ________

calf [6] ________

weight ________

THINGS TO IMPROVE:

THINK OF 3 GOOD THINGS THAT HAPPENED THIS WEEK:

DAY 36

__/__/__

How I feel today:

○ ☹ ○ 😐 ○ ☺

START WITH GRATITUDE

Today I am grateful about...

PRIORITY GOALS

If you talked to your friends the way you talked to your body, you'd have no friends left at all. – MARCIA HUTCHINSON

BREAKFAST

LUNCH

WATER

SLEEP TIME

The words you say to yourself can either motivate you toward your goals, or seriously stall your progress, or prevent you from starting on your journey. Be kind to yourself.

DINNER

SNACKS

Name something you LOVE ABOUT YOUR BODY *that isn't related to what it looks like.*

EXERCISE / ACTIVITY

DAY 37

___/___/___

How I feel today:

○ ☹ ○ 😐 ○ ☺

START WITH GRATITUDE

Today I am grateful about...

PRIORITY GOALS

Instead of being ashamed of what you've been through, be proud of what you have overcome!

– PHIL MCGRAW

BREAKFAST

LUNCH

WATER

SLEEP TIME

Think of a time you were
PROUD OF YOURSELF
What happened and how did you feel?

DINNER

SNACKS

EXERCISE / ACTIVITY

DAY 38

__/__/__

How I feel today:

○ ☹ ○ 😐 ○ ☺

START WITH GRATITUDE

Today I am grateful about...

PRIORITY GOALS

*To be beautiful means to be yourself.
You don't need to be accepted by others.
You need to accept yourself.*

– THICH NHAT HANH

BREAKFAST

LUNCH

WATER

SLEEP TIME

DINNER

SNACKS

What is your biggest struggle with LIKING YOURSELF? *What can you do about it?*

EXERCISE / ACTIVITY

DAY 39

__/__/__

How I feel today:

START WITH GRATITUDE

Today I am grateful about...

PRIORITY GOALS

You are beautiful no matter what they say. Words can't bring you down.

– CHRISTINA AGUILERA / LINDA PERRY

BREAKFAST

LUNCH

WATER

DINNER

SNACKS

SLEEP TIME

Give yourself 5 genuine COMPLIMENTS.

EXERCISE / ACTIVITY

DAY 40

__/__/__

How I feel today:

○ ☹ ○ 😐 ○ ☺

START WITH GRATITUDE

Today I am grateful about...

PRIORITY GOALS

Good company in a journey makes the way seem shorter.

\- IZAAK WALTON

WATER

BREAKFAST

LUNCH

SLEEP TIME

DINNER

SNACKS

Who are the people whose COMPANY YOU ENJOYED *today?*

EXERCISE / ACTIVITY

DAY 41

___/___/___

How I feel today:

○ ☹ ○ 😐 ○ ☺

START WITH GRATITUDE

Today I am grateful about...

PRIORITY GOALS

If you continuously compete with others, you become bitter, but if you continuously compete with yourself, you become better.

BREAKFAST

LUNCH

WATER

SLEEP TIME

DINNER

SNACKS

It is one thing to have a good company for your journey for support and inspiration, and an entirely different thing is to enter a competition with them or compare your results to theirs. Everyone has their own motivations and limitations.

Set your own pace and

Compare YOURSELF ONLY TO Yourself

EXERCISE / ACTIVITY

DAY 42

__/__/__

How I feel today:

○ ☹ ○ 😐 ○ ☺

START WITH GRATITUDE

Today I am grateful about...

PRIORITY GOALS

Keep on smiling!

You Look So much Better when You Smile

Try to KEEP A SMILE *on your face for as much of the day as possible. Then, write about your experience.*

BREAKFAST

LUNCH

DINNER

SNACKS

EXERCISE / ACTIVITY

WATER

SLEEP TIME

THIS WEEK'S REFLECTION

WRITE YOURSELF A LOVE LETTER.

That's right. A love letter.

This is one of the most effective methods to practice self-love and a great tool that can calm and center you in times of crisis when everything seems upside down. You can read it anytime you need a little nudge to get up and move on.

Love yourself first and everything else falls into line.

– LUCILLE BALL

arm [1] ....

chest [2] ....

waist [3] ....

hips [4] ....

thigh [5] ....

calf [6] ....

weight ....

How to write your love letter?

» Don't type. There are proven psychological benefits to writing things down by hand.

» Start with a salutation that will make you smile.

» Include affirmative sentences about your character, body, goals, achievements, values, etc.

» And finally, don't be shy or modest and forget about your insecurities. Everyone is worthy of love. You don't need anyone's approval (even yours) to deserve that love.

THINGS TO IMPROVE:

THINK OF 3 GOOD THINGS THAT HAPPENED THIS WEEK:

DAY 43

___/___/___

How I feel today:

START WITH GRATITUDE

Today I am grateful about...

PRIORITY GOALS

You don't have to necessarily have done anything wrong for things to get completely out of control.

– JORDAN PETERSON

BREAKFAST

LUNCH

DINNER

SNACKS

EXERCISE / ACTIVITY

Don't blame or feel sorry for yourself for the struggles in your life. Stand up in the face of the things you are afraid of. Those challenges between you and your goals will only make you stronger if you dare to face them.

This week try do something you have been
AVOIDING FOR A LONG TIME.

WATER

SLEEP TIME

DAY 44

___/___/___

How I feel today:

START WITH GRATITUDE

Today I am grateful about...

PRIORITY GOALS

Fall down 7 times, get up 8.

BREAKFAST

LUNCH

WATER

SLEEP TIME

Forget about being consistent all the time. It is impossible to not fall off the wagon from time to time. Sometimes you fall off the wagon for months and have to restart 100 times. But it is okay.

DINNER

SNACKS

EXERCISE / ACTIVITY

You CAN do this!

Just focus on getting back on the wagon as fast as you can.

DAY 45

___/___/___

How I feel today:

○  ○  ○ 

START WITH GRATITUDE

Today I am grateful about...

PRIORITY GOALS

Motivation is what gets you started. Habit is what keeps you going.

– JIM RYUN

WATER

BREAKFAST

LUNCH

SLEEP TIME

Making the decision to change your life for the better is only the first step of the journey. That step means nothing unless you form good habits.

Whether you have a new post-holiday fitness goal, or want to try a different career, it can be exhausting to maintain the motivation to work towards your goals. However, develop good habits, and they will operate automatically to take you step by step closer to your desired outcome.

DINNER

SNACKS

EXERCISE / ACTIVITY

What is one

HABIT YOU WANT TO START?

DAY 46

___/___/___

How I feel today:

○ ☹ ○ 😐 ○ ☺

START WITH GRATITUDE

Today I am grateful about...

PRIORITY GOALS

A small leak sinks a great ship.

- BENJAMIN FRANKLIN

WATER

SLEEP TIME

BREAKFAST

LUNCH

DINNER

SNACKS

We are creatures of habit. Habits either help to propel us forward or to hinder our progress in life.

EXERCISE / ACTIVITY

What is one

HABIT YOU SHOULD BREAK?

DAY 47

__/__/__

How I feel today:

START WITH GRATITUDE

Today I am grateful about...

PRIORITY GOALS

Never stop learning!

BREAKFAST

LUNCH

WATER

SLEEP TIME

Educate yourself and learn something new every single day. It doesn't matter how you will do it – through a podcast, an online course, an audiobook, a video tutorial on YouTube, TED Talks or other means. This is one habit that can do wonders for your self-confidence.

DINNER

SNACKS

EXERCISE / ACTIVITY

What skills do you want to
LEARN OR IMPROVE?

DAY 48

__/__/__

How I feel today:

○ ☹ ○ 😐 ○ ☺

START WITH GRATITUDE

Today I am grateful about...

PRIORITY GOALS

Strength does not come from winning. Your struggles develop your strengths. When you go through great hardships and decide not to surrender, that is a strength.

– ARNOLD SCHWARZENEGGER

BREAKFAST

LUNCH

WATER

SLEEP TIME

DINNER

SNACKS

You are stronger than you think

EXERCISE / ACTIVITY

Can you remember a
NEGATIVE EVENT
that led to
POSITIVE CHANGES
in your life?

DAY 49

___/___/___

How I feel today:

○ ☹ ○ 😐 ○ ☺

START WITH GRATITUDE

Today I am grateful about...

PRIORITY GOALS

Someday is not a day of the week.

WATER

SLEEP TIME

BREAKFAST

LUNCH

Often times we ignore unpleasant tasks in favor of something enjoyable that gives us a temporary mood boost. Such procrastination is often followed by shame and guilt and causes us to miss out on achieving our goals.

One way to fight procrastination is to break down tasks into smaller, easily accomplished steps. Then, instead of "just do it," which can be overwhelming, we can focus on

just get started.

DINNER

SNACKS

EXERCISE / ACTIVITY

Break down one of your main goals into

3 SMALLER GOALS

THIS WEEK'S REFLECTION

CONFRONT YOUR FEARS

Immersed in fear – of failure, of success, or of not being perfect – sometimes we are so worried and nervous that we choose to procrastinate or not take action at all.

Breaking through your fears is probably one of the most important habits that you could develop.

It requires regular practice to let your brain become accustomed to fear. Gradually face your fears, in small doses that don't overwhelm you.

Get used to doing one thing that makes you feel uncomfortable each and every single day.

Talk to a stranger, give someone a compliment, ask a question that you think will make you look naive, or tell someone the truth about something that makes you feel uncomfortable.

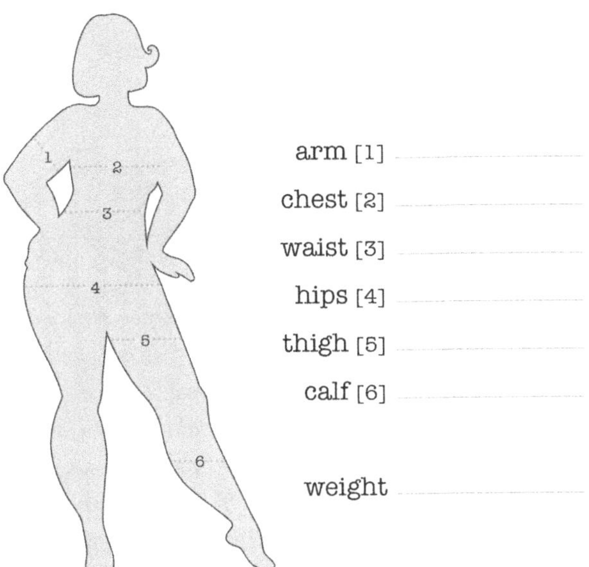

UNCOMFORTABLE THINGS TO TRY:

THINK OF 3 GOOD THINGS THAT HAPPENED THIS WEEK:

DAY 50

___/___/___

START WITH GRATITUDE

Today I am grateful about...

To grow yourself,
you must know yourself.

– JOHN C. MAXWELL

BREAKFAST

LUNCH

DINNER

SNACKS

EXERCISE / ACTIVITY

How I feel today:

PRIORITY GOALS

You can only improve that which you are aware of. What are your strengths? Your weaknesses? Your personal values? Your needs? How can you know what to aim for if you don't know the answers to these questions?

This week take the time to
get to know yourself.

Spend 10 "think minutes" each day
in complete silence to reflect and dissect your thoughts and feelings.

WATER

SLEEP TIME

DAY 51

___/___/___

How I feel today:

○ ☹ ○ 😐 ○ ☺

START WITH GRATITUDE

Today I am grateful about...

PRIORITY GOALS

Who are you?

BREAKFAST

LUNCH

DESCRIBE YOURSELF

using the first 5 words that come to your mind.

DINNER

SNACKS

List 5 words that

YOU'D LIKE TO USE

to describe yourself.

EXERCISE / ACTIVITY

WATER

SLEEP TIME

DAY 52

___/___/___

START WITH GRATITUDE
Today I am grateful about...

How I feel today:

PRIORITY GOALS

It's not hard to make decisions, once you know what your values are.

– ROY E. DISNEY

WATER

BREAKFAST

LUNCH

SLEEP TIME

If we don't know what is truly meaningful to us, we can easily end up pursuing someone else's idea of success and happy life, taking decisions that leave us feeling miserable.

DINNER

SNACKS

What are the principles you want to live by?

HONESTY
KINDNESS
LOYALTY
COURAGE
AUTHENTICITY
etc.

EXERCISE / ACTIVITY

Be mindful, there is a difference between our values and what we care about.
For example, you may care about wealth but if you value honesty and integrity, you may still decline a high paying job that involves questionable practices.

DAY 53

__/__/__

How I feel today:

○ ☹ ○ 😐 ○ ☺

START WITH GRATITUDE

Today I am grateful about...

PRIORITY GOALS

If you feel like there's something out there that you're supposed to be doing, if you have a passion for it, then stop wishing and just do it.

– WANDA SKYES

WATER

BREAKFAST

LUNCH

SLEEP TIME

What could you talk about for 30 minutes with absolutely no preparation?

DINNER

SNACKS

If you had to leave your house all day, every day, where would you go and what would you do?

EXERCISE / ACTIVITY

Finish this sentence: "My life would be incomplete without ..."

DAY 54

___/___/___

How I feel today:

○  ○  ○ 

START WITH GRATITUDE

Today I am grateful about...

PRIORITY GOALS

The two most important days in life are the day you are born and the day you find out why.

BREAKFAST

LUNCH

WATER

SLEEP TIME

DINNER

SNACKS

EXERCISE / ACTIVITY

Most of us don't have a clue what we want to do with our lives. Even after we finish school, get a job and start a family.

It might help to figure it out if you imagine yourself when you are 90 years old and ask yourself:

What is your biggest regret?

What is true about yourself today that will make your 8-year-old self sad?

How do you want to be remembered?

DAY 55

___/___/___

How I feel today:

○ ☹ ○ 😐 ○ ☺

START WITH GRATITUDE

Today I am grateful about...

PRIORITY GOALS

We cannot become what we want by remaining what we are.

– MAX DE PREE

BREAKFAST

LUNCH

WATER

SLEEP TIME

DINNER

SNACKS

Change can be scary but that fear can only hold us back. Overcoming it is a huge part of any transformation.

EXERCISE / ACTIVITY

DAY 56

___/___/___

How I feel today:

○ ☹ ○ 😐 ○ ☺

START WITH GRATITUDE

Today I am grateful about...

PRIORITY GOALS

Where words fail, music speaks.

– HANS CHRISTIAN ANDERSEN

WATER

BREAKFAST

LUNCH

SLEEP TIME

If you had to name a
SONG FOR YOUR CURRENT LIFE,
which one would it be?

DINNER

SNACKS

Why?

EXERCISE / ACTIVITY

If you could change things around, what would you want your main song to be?

THIS WEEK'S REFLECTION

KNOW WHO YOU ARE

Take time to know what you like, what you don't, your needs, your values, your standards, your goals, your strengths and weaknesses, what you cannot tolerate and what the essentials in your life are.

Only then you can learn to accept who you are and live your life authentically.

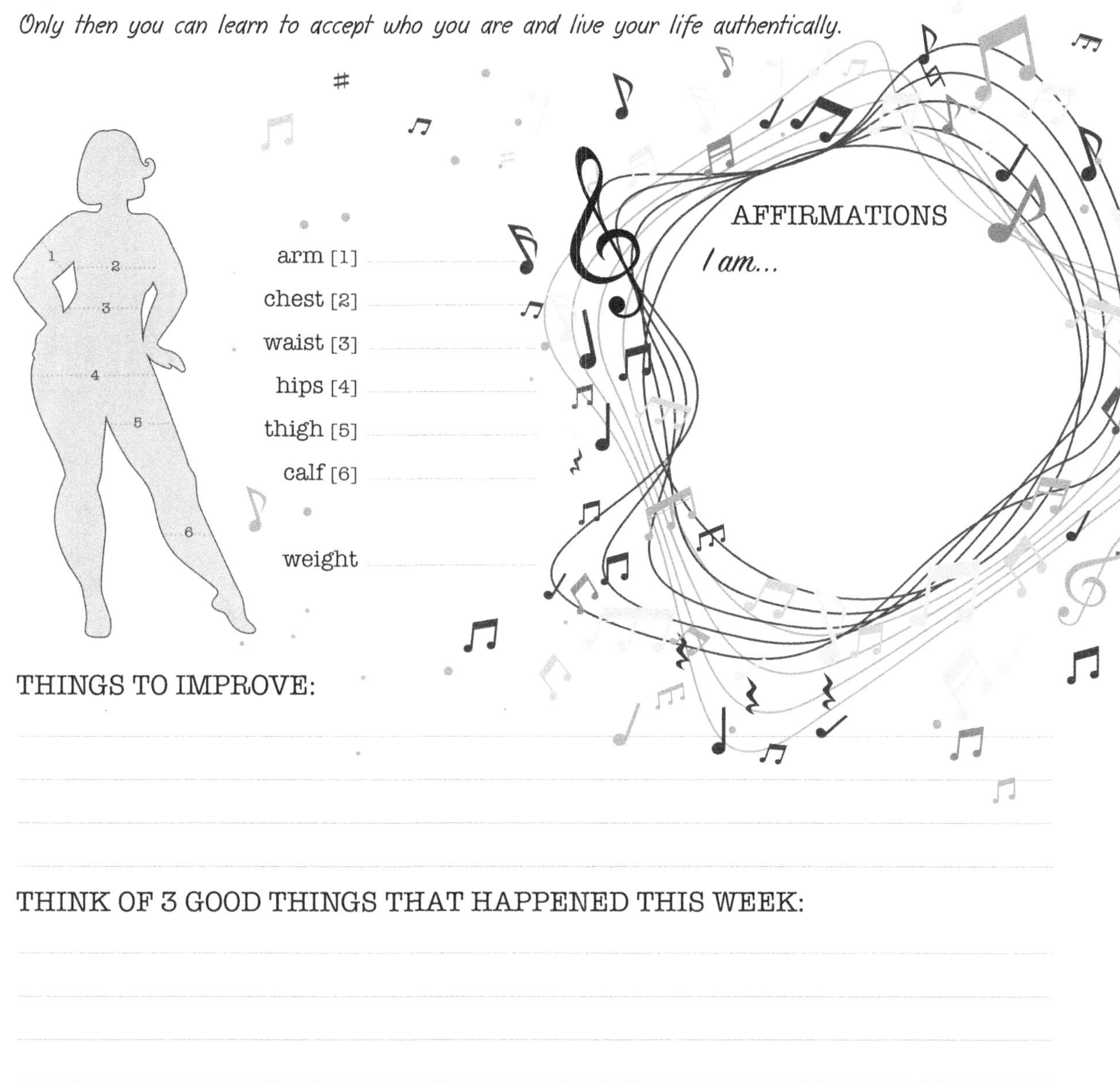

arm [1] ____________

chest [2] ____________

waist [3] ____________

hips [4] ____________

thigh [5] ____________

calf [6] ____________

weight ____________

THINGS TO IMPROVE:

____

____

____

THINK OF 3 GOOD THINGS THAT HAPPENED THIS WEEK:

____

____

____

____

____

DAY 57

___/___/___

How I feel today:

○  ○  ○ 

START WITH GRATITUDE

Today I am grateful about...

PRIORITY GOALS

It is impossible to make everyone like you. Don't be defined by those who don't!

BREAKFAST

LUNCH

WATER

SLEEP TIME

DINNER

SNACKS

EXERCISE / ACTIVITY

When someone criticizes you there is a real risk that their opinion gets into your head and guides how you see yourself.

The moment you realize that you are not defined by the opinion of someone who does not like you or know you, that is the moment when you will regain your power and be ***free to be yourself.***

DAY 58

___/___/___

How I feel today:

○ ☹ ○ 😐 ○ ☺

START WITH GRATITUDE

Today I am grateful about...

PRIORITY GOALS

The company you keep is a reflection of how you feel about yourself.

BREAKFAST

LUNCH

WATER

SLEEP TIME

DINNER

SNACKS

Love yourself enough to surround yourself with people who respect and support you just as you are.

EXERCISE / ACTIVITY

Who is your FAVORITE PERSON *in the world?*

DAY 59

___/___/___

How I feel today:

○ ☹ ○ 😐 ○ ☺

START WITH GRATITUDE

Today I am grateful about...

PRIORITY GOALS

No one can make you feel inferior without your consent.

– ELEANOR ROOSEVELT

WATER

BREAKFAST

LUNCH

SLEEP TIME

We cannot stop other people from careless, disrespectful, rude or even cruel behavior, but we can stop ourselves from reacting to it.

DINNER

SNACKS

EXERCISE / ACTIVITY

DAY 60

__/__/__

How I feel today:

○ ☹ ○ 😐 ○ ☺

START WITH GRATITUDE

Today I am grateful about...

PRIORITY GOALS

You didn't come this far to only come this far.

BREAKFAST

LUNCH

WATER

SLEEP TIME

60 days since you started your journey but who is counting. Surely there have been ups and downs, mistakes, and moments of pride and joy.

You are doing great!

DINNER

SNACKS

EXERCISE / ACTIVITY

keep on going

DAY 61

__/__/__

How I feel today:

○ ☹ ○ 😐 ○ ☺

START WITH GRATITUDE

Today I am grateful about...

PRIORITY GOALS

Don't be afraid to share your thoughts and opinions.

BREAKFAST

LUNCH

WATER

SLEEP TIME

Drop the assumption that everyone else is judging you and remember:

» No one can determine or diminish your core value as a person. Period.

» Everything becomes a past, even your embarrassment and humiliation.

DINNER

SNACKS

EXERCISE / ACTIVITY

DAY 62

___/___/___

START WITH GRATITUDE

Today I am grateful about...

How I feel today:

PRIORITY GOALS

Learn to say NO

It can be hard to say no, but you should value enough your time and needs to do it when a request conflicts with them.

BREAKFAST

LUNCH

DINNER

SNACKS

EXERCISE / ACTIVITY

WATER

SLEEP TIME

When should we say no? Ask yourself:

» Will saying yes prevent me from focusing on something that's more important?

» Does this request align with my values?

When was the last time you said yes when you should have said NO?

It is time to get better at saying no.

DAY 63

___/___/___

How I feel today:

START WITH GRATITUDE

Today I am grateful about...

PRIORITY GOALS

Be yourself. Everyone else is already taken.

BREAKFAST

LUNCH

WATER

SLEEP TIME

DINNER

SNACKS

EXERCISE / ACTIVITY

WOMAN YOU ARE AMAZING!

THIS WEEK'S REFLECTION

ALWAYS BE TRUE TO YOURSELF

The need of approval has become such a big part of our lives that it is getting harder and harder to let ourselves show the Real Me. It seems easier to just go with the flow and, like a true people pleaser, be like a chameleon and comply with other people's opinions, feelings and needs.

But if you want to live your life the way you want, you need to learn to be honest with yourself and others about what you think, feel, want, and need.

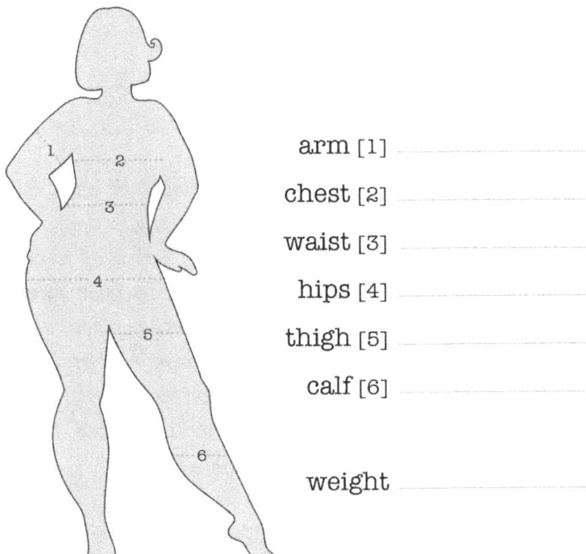

Learn how to be true to yourself.

» Start with knowing who you are and accepting yourself. Know your passions, strengths, and limitations.

» Shake off the urge to seek approval from everyone.

» Surround yourself with people who respect you just as you are.

» Share your thoughts and opinions freely.

» Honor your time, needs and values, and say no to requests that conflict with them.

» Believe that you are enough just as you are.

THINGS TO IMPROVE:

THINK OF 3 GOOD THINGS THAT HAPPENED THIS WEEK:

DAY 64

___/___/___

How I feel today:

○  ○  ○ 

START WITH GRATITUDE

Today I am grateful about...

PRIORITY GOALS

Make time for yourself.

One habit that most of us fail to acknowledge is implementing some "me time" in our lives.

Do one small thing that you enjoy doing every single day. It is essential for your peace of mind. Whether you listen to your favorite music, read a book you love, watch a movie, write in your journal, or anything else for that matter, be sure to set aside some time for yourself in the day.

BREAKFAST

LUNCH

DINNER

SNACKS

WATER

SLEEP TIME

EXERCISE / ACTIVITY

What SELF-CARE ACTIVITIES *bring you feelings of joy and calm?*

DAY 65

___/___/___

START WITH GRATITUDE

Today I am grateful about...

How I feel today:

PRIORITY GOALS

Make your body happy.

It is important to make that gorgeous body of yours happy and energized. Work up a sweat and do some yoga, or running, or simply unleash your inner Beyonce on the dance floor.

BREAKFAST

LUNCH

DINNER

SNACKS

EXERCISE / ACTIVITY

As Vicki Baum once said,

"There are shortcuts to happiness and dancing is one of them!"

WATER

SLEEP TIME

DAY 66

/ /

How I feel today:

PRIORITY GOALS

START WITH GRATITUDE

Today I am grateful about...

Coloring is a healthy way to relieve stress.

BREAKFAST

LUNCH

DINNER

SNACKS

Not only does coloring make you feel like a kid again, but it is also a great way to relax your brain and quiet your restless mind.

EXERCISE / ACTIVITY

WATER

SLEEP TIME

DAY 67

/ /

How I feel today:

START WITH GRATITUDE

Today I am grateful about...

PRIORITY GOALS

Color your way to a good mood!

BREAKFAST

LUNCH

DINNER

SNACKS

EXERCISE / ACTIVITY

WATER

SLEEP TIME

DAY 68

__/__/__

How I feel today:

START WITH GRATITUDE

Today I am grateful about...

PRIORITY GOALS

A true friend accepts who you are, but also helps you become who you should be.

WATER

BREAKFAST

LUNCH

SLEEP TIME

DINNER

SNACKS

EXERCISE / ACTIVITY

If you cannot meet in person, pick up the phone and
CONNECT WITH A GOOD FRIEND
for a quick dose of happiness.

DAY 69

__/__/__

How I feel today:

○ ☹ ○ 😐 ○ ☺

START WITH GRATITUDE

Today I am grateful about...

PRIORITY GOALS

Life is meant for good friends and great adventures.

WATER

BREAKFAST

LUNCH

SLEEP TIME

DINNER

SNACKS

EXERCISE / ACTIVITY

If you could TRAVEL ANYWHERE *in the world for any length of time, where would it be?*

DAY 70

___/___/___

START WITH GRATITUDE

Today I am grateful about...

PRIORITY GOALS

How I feel today:

Being sexy is all about attitude, not body type. It's a state of mind.

– AMISHA PATEL

BREAKFAST

LUNCH

DINNER

SNACKS

WATER

SLEEP TIME

EXERCISE / ACTIVITY

It doesn't matter whether you are going out or staying home for the day. Put on your favorite clothes, do your hair and makeup and do it for yourself.

Feel sexy today.

THIS WEEK'S REFLECTION

It is time to

PLAN YOUR DATE WITH YOURSELF.

Make this the month when you take yourself out on a date.

When was the last time you had alone time outside of your partner, friends, and family?

Taking yourself on a date can be empowering, uplifting, and do miracles for your mind and acceptance. This is one of the most effective and fun ways to practice self-love and

you deserve it!

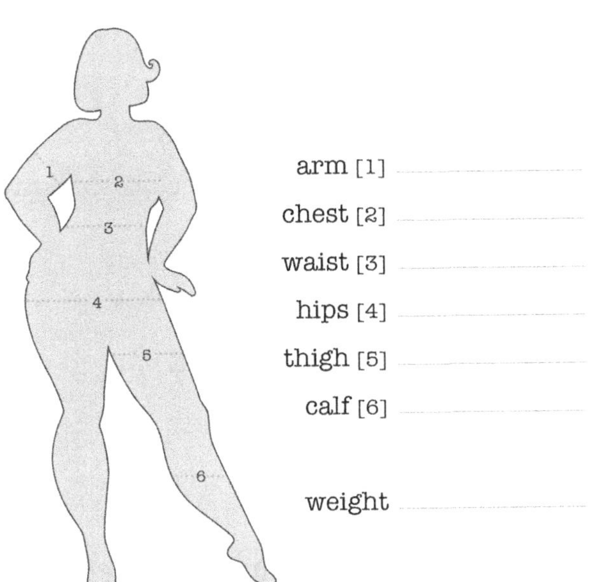

Plan your date.

» *Choose an activity that you think you will truly enjoy. You may go out for dinner and a movie, book a spa treatment, take yourself on a picnic, or go for a walk.*

» *Put your solo date on your calendar and make sure to show up. Don't ghost yourself!*

» *Get dressed up and do whatever you need to do to feel good about yourself.*

» *Treat it like you would treat any date with another person. Make it special!*

THINGS TO IMPROVE:

THINK OF 3 GOOD THINGS THAT HAPPENED THIS WEEK:

DAY 71

__ / __ / __

START WITH GRATITUDE

Today I am grateful about...

How I feel today:

○  ○  ○ 

PRIORITY GOALS

Believe in yourself.

BREAKFAST

LUNCH

WATER

SLEEP TIME

DINNER

SNACKS

EXERCISE / ACTIVITY

No one can tell you who you are and what you are made of. Only you yourself know what you are made of, and only you yourself can do the work to become who you want to be.

– MARISKA HARGITAY

DAY 72

/ /

How I feel today:

START WITH GRATITUDE

Today I am grateful about...

PRIORITY GOALS

Eliminate self-doubt.

BREAKFAST

LUNCH

WATER

SLEEP TIME

DINNER

SNACKS

EXERCISE / ACTIVITY

We all experience feelings of self-doubt, especially in the face of a major event or change in our life. Negative thoughts start flooding our mind, like "Maybe I shouldn't do this", or "It is not going to work anyway", or "It is not even that big of a deal, a lot of people have a job they don't like", or "I don't deserve something better".

The first step towards a better life is to eliminate these negative beliefs and replace them with empowering ones.

DAY 73

___/___/___

How I feel today:

○ ☹ ○ 😐 ○ ☺

START WITH GRATITUDE

Today I am grateful about...

PRIORITY GOALS

Trade your expectations for appreciation.

WATER

BREAKFAST

LUNCH

SLEEP TIME

If you search for your happiness in outside changes and events, you may never be happy if they don't happen the way you expect. Instead of waiting for the outside world to bring you happiness, find it within you by appreciating what you have.

DINNER

SNACKS

Think of one of your goals and the work you have put into pursuing it, whether successfully or not. Now ***remember those moments along the way when*** **YOU FELT JOY OR SATISFACTION** ***from what you were doing.***

EXERCISE / ACTIVITY

DAY 74

/ /

How I feel today:

START WITH GRATITUDE

Today I am grateful about...

PRIORITY GOALS

Don't cry because it's over. Smile because it happened.

WATER

BREAKFAST

LUNCH

SLEEP TIME

A happy moment can last a lifetime if you remember to smile when you think of it.

DINNER

SNACKS

What are the things you want to REMEMBER FROM TODAY?

EXERCISE / ACTIVITY

DAY 75

__/__/__

How I feel today:

START WITH GRATITUDE

Today I am grateful about...

PRIORITY GOALS

Keep working on your New Me not because your Old Me is bad but because your New Me is better.

BREAKFAST

LUNCH

WATER

SLEEP TIME

DINNER

SNACKS

What are your GREATEST STRENGTHS?

EXERCISE / ACTIVITY

Which ones can you IMPROVE EVEN FURTHER?

DAY 76

___/___/___

How I feel today:

○ ☹ ○ 😐 ○ ☺

START WITH GRATITUDE

Today I am grateful about...

PRIORITY GOALS

This page breezes in to tell you that
you are doing great!

BREAKFAST

LUNCH

WATER

SLEEP TIME

DINNER

SNACKS

Take care of yourself in a healthy way.

Rest if needed.

Chasing after your goals is admirable but know that

YOU ARE
enough
always,
regardless of the results.

EXERCISE / ACTIVITY

DAY 77

___/___/___

How I feel today:

○ ☹ ○ 😐 ○ ☺

START WITH GRATITUDE

Today I am grateful about...

PRIORITY GOALS

It's not what you are that holds you back, it's what you think you are not.

– DENIS WAITLEY

BREAKFAST

LUNCH

WATER

SLEEP TIME

We often hold back from doing things because we think "I can't do that", or "That's not for me", or above all "I am not [smart / pretty / consistent / motivated / adventurous / etc.] enough to do it".

We are held back by the very limits we set for ourselves.

Trust yourself, you know and can more than you think you do.

DINNER

SNACKS

EXERCISE / ACTIVITY

THIS WEEK'S REFLECTION

YOU ARE GOOD ENOUGH.

Get it through your head that it doesn't matter how you look, how many wrinkles you have, much you are overweight, how many dimples there are on your thighs. It doesn't matter that you are overly sensitive, socially awkward, irrational at times, terrible at math, not environment friendly enough, or that you make mistakes. YOU ARE STILL GOOD ENOUGH.

You are imperfect and you are wired for struggle but you are worthy of love and belonging.

– BRENÉ BROWN

1 2 3 4 5 6

arm [1] ....

chest [2] ....

waist [3] ....

hips [4] ....

thigh [5] ....

calf [6] ....

weight ....

Fill in the blanks:

It doesn't matter that ....

I AM STILL ENOUGH!

It doesn't matter that ....

I AM STILL ENOUGH!

It doesn't matter that ....

I AM STILL ENOUGH!

It doesn't matter that ....

I AM STILL ENOUGH!

It doesn't matter that ....

I AM STILL ENOUGH!

THINGS TO IMPROVE:

THINK OF 3 GOOD THINGS THAT HAPPENED THIS WEEK:

DAY 78

___/___/___

How I feel today:

START WITH GRATITUDE

Today I am grateful about...

PRIORITY GOALS

Be healthy to be happy.

BREAKFAST

LUNCH

WATER

SLEEP TIME

DINNER

SNACKS

You can have good looks, wealth and success, but will you be able to enjoy any of it if you don't have your health?

What can you start doing right now to PURSUE GOOD HEALTH?

EXERCISE / ACTIVITY

DAY 79

__/__/__

How I feel today:

○ ☹ ○ 😐 ○ ☺

START WITH GRATITUDE

Today I am grateful about...

PRIORITY GOALS

Be happy to be healthy.

BREAKFAST

LUNCH

WATER

SLEEP TIME

Research shows that higher levels of well-being (i.e., happiness) contribute to better general health, better immune system functioning, reduced susceptibility to colds and flu viruses, and fewer chronic conditions such as heart disease and diabetes.

DINNER

SNACKS

Health and happiness go hand in hand.

EXERCISE / ACTIVITY

DAY 80

___/___/___

How I feel today:

○ ☹ ○ 😐 ○ ☺

START WITH GRATITUDE

Today I am grateful about...

PRIORITY GOALS

Yesterday is history. Tomorrow is a mystery.
Today is a gift. That is why it is called the present.

BREAKFAST

LUNCH

WATER

SLEEP TIME

DINNER

SNACKS

Learn to focus only on the present.

Close your eyes.
Identify and list
EVERY SOUND
THAT YOU HEAR
over the span of 2 minutes.

EXERCISE / ACTIVITY

DAY 81

/ /

How I feel today:

○ ☹ ○ 😐 ○ ☺

START WITH GRATITUDE

Today I am grateful about...

PRIORITY GOALS

There is beauty all around us.

BREAKFAST

LUNCH

WATER

SLEEP TIME

DINNER

SNACKS

Often, we are so caught up in our everyday lives that we fail to take it in. Consciously observe your surroundings and notice the beauty around you.

Name
3 BEAUTIFUL THINGS
that you saw today.

EXERCISE / ACTIVITY

DAY 82

___ / ___ / ___

How I feel today:

○ ☹ ○ 😐 ○ ☺

START WITH GRATITUDE

Today I am grateful about...

PRIORITY GOALS

A good laugh and a long sleep are the best cures for anything.

BREAKFAST

LUNCH

WATER

SLEEP TIME

How do you

RELAX, REST, AND UNPLUG?

DINNER

SNACKS

What is something that always

MAKES YOU LAUGH?

EXERCISE / ACTIVITY

DAY 83

___/___/___

How I feel today:

START WITH GRATITUDE

Today I am grateful about...

PRIORITY GOALS

Nature always wears the colors of the spirit.

– RALPH WALDO EMERSON

BREAKFAST

LUNCH

WATER

SLEEP TIME

Research shows that spending time in nature, or enjoying pockets of green in urban settings, has been found to reduce stress and negative emotions, and help with mental health problems such as anxiety and depression.

DINNER

SNACKS

EXERCISE / ACTIVITY

Get outside for some green time!

Or create your own green space by planting some flowers or your own vegetables, which can have a similar effect.

DAY 84

___/___/___

How I feel today:

○ ☹ ○ 😐 ○ ☺

START WITH GRATITUDE

Today I am grateful about...

PRIORITY GOALS

Exercise to be fit, not skinny.
Eat to nourish your body.

WATER

BREAKFAST

LUNCH

SLEEP TIME

How does
EXERCISE AFFECT
YOUR MOOD?
Can you tell a difference on the days you exercise?

DINNER

SNACKS

EXERCISE / ACTIVITY

What
FOOD DO YOU ENJOY
that is also healthy?

THIS WEEK'S REFLECTION

MAKE HEALTHY CHOICES FOR YOUR LIFESTYLE.

Good health is absolutely essential for leading a productive life.

Treat your body like a temple, not a woodshed. The mind and body work together. Your body needs to be a good support system for the mind and spirit.

– JIM ROHN

1
2
3
4
5
6

arm [1] ____

chest [2] ____

waist [3] ____

hips [4] ____

thigh [5] ____

calf [6] ____

weight ____

- *Eat nutritious foods.*
- *Be physically active.*
- *Get enough sleep.*
- *Focus on your mental health.*

It can be overwhelming to do it all, so start small. Focus on one healthy habit at a time. Once you get one healthy habit down, move onto the next.

THINGS TO IMPROVE:

THINK OF 3 GOOD THINGS THAT HAPPENED THIS WEEK:

DAY 85

___/___/___

START WITH GRATITUDE

Today I am grateful about...

How I feel today:

○  ○  ○ 

PRIORITY GOALS

This is a reminder that you are strong, beautiful, and kind, and can handle anything this week throws at you.

BREAKFAST

LUNCH

WATER

SLEEP TIME

Remember something you accomplished, even though YOU DOUBTED *you would be able to.*

DINNER

SNACKS

EXERCISE / ACTIVITY

Remember a moment when you didn't feel like doing something BUT DID IT ANYWAY.

DAY 86

__/__/__

START WITH GRATITUDE

Today I am grateful about...

How I feel today:

○  ○  ○ 

PRIORITY GOALS

Be a rainbow in someone's cloud.

WATER

BREAKFAST

LUNCH

SLEEP TIME

Take the time to be kind today. You can make all the difference in someone's day. You can simply smile, or show warmth to someone. You can give someone your time and truly listen to what they have to say. You can choose not to judge.

DINNER

SNACKS

Who or what inspires you to be A BETTER PERSON?

EXERCISE / ACTIVITY

What could you do today to MAKE ANOTHER PERSON FEEL BETTER?

DAY 87

/ /

How I feel today:

START WITH GRATITUDE

Today I am grateful about...

PRIORITY GOALS

Get it all OUT

WATER

BREAKFAST

LUNCH

SLEEP TIME

If you could say anything to anyone, what would you say?

This is your chance to be brutally honest. Do you want to tell someone how much they have affected your life? Tell a co-worker that they do a crappy job?

You can safely get it all out here:

DINNER

SNACKS

EXERCISE / ACTIVITY

DAY 88

___/___/___

How I feel today:

○ ☹ ○ 😐 ○ ☺

START WITH GRATITUDE

Today I am grateful about...

PRIORITY GOALS

Remember you have been criticizing yourself for years and it hasn't worked. Try approving of yourself and see what happens.

– LOUISE HAY

BREAKFAST

LUNCH

WATER

SLEEP TIME

DINNER

SNACKS

We should always strive for kindness, and this includes how we treat ourselves.

EXERCISE / ACTIVITY

Write something

SOMETHING POSITIVE ABOUT YOURSELF.

DAY 89

__/__/__

How I feel today:

START WITH GRATITUDE

Today I am grateful about...

PRIORITY GOALS

You can give without loving,
but you cannot love without giving.
Giving is part of how we show love.

WATER

BREAKFAST

LUNCH

SLEEP TIME

DINNER

SNACKS

Think of a time when someone showed you such
GENEROSITY
that you thought, "Wow, I can't believe they did that for me."

EXERCISE / ACTIVITY

DAY 90

___/___/___

START WITH GRATITUDE

Today I am grateful about...

How I feel today:

PRIORITY GOALS

No act of kindness,
no matter how small,
is ever wasted.

– AESOP

WATER

BREAKFAST

LUNCH

SLEEP TIME

Research shows that when we are kind to others, we are healthier and happier. Random acts of kindness make us feel good, as our bodies respond by producing the "happiness" chemicals dopamine, endorphins and oxytocin. They are good for our health too, as they help decrease stress, which is associated with a variety of health problems.

DINNER

SNACKS

How can you HELP SOMEONE *who's less fortunate than yourself?*

EXERCISE / ACTIVITY

DAY 91

___/___/___

How I feel today:

○ ☹ ○ 😐 ○ ☺

START WITH GRATITUDE

Today I am grateful about...

PRIORITY GOALS

Be kind to yourself.

BREAKFAST

LUNCH

DINNER

SNACKS

EXERCISE / ACTIVITY

» *Don't just be good to others. Be good to yourself too.*

» *Love yourself as much as you want to be loved.*

» *Respect yourself as much as you want to be respected.*

How you treat yourself is how you are inviting the world to treat you.

WATER

SLEEP TIME

THIS WEEK'S REFLECTION

BE KIND TO YOUR MIND.

It is hard to stay strong, happy and hopeful, and love yourself 100% of the time, when hard times hit. Especially when it is your own mind that is being unkind to you. It is easy to get lost in the negative self-talk spiral when you feel down.

Don't beat yourself up for your negative feelings and emotions. They are something you experience; they don't define you. Remember,

you walk in the rain,
and you feel the rain,
but you are not the rain.

arm [1] ____________

chest [2] ____________

waist [3] ____________

hips [4] ____________

thigh [5] ____________

calf [6] ____________

weight ____________

Living in a world where people make New Year's resolutions to lose weight, hit the gym, and eat healthier, spend a little time thinking about your mind that does so much work.

THINGS TO IMPROVE:

____

____

____

____

THINK OF 3 GOOD THINGS THAT HAPPENED THIS WEEK:

____

____

____

____

____

DAY 92

/ /

How I feel today:

○  ○  ○ ☺

START WITH GRATITUDE

Today I am grateful about...

PRIORITY GOALS

No matter how you feel today, get up, dress up and show up!

BREAKFAST

LUNCH

DINNER

SNACKS

WATER

SLEEP TIME

EXERCISE / ACTIVITY

We all have bad days and we can find a thousand excuses not to do something. Don't give up on yourself. Accept that it might not be your most productive day but get up anyway, put your game face on and do your best. Some progress is better than none.

DAY 93

/ /

How I feel today:

START WITH GRATITUDE

Today I am grateful about...

PRIORITY GOALS

The more you trust your intuition, the more empowered you become, the stronger you become, and the happier you become.

– GISELE BUNDCHEN

BREAKFAST

LUNCH

WATER

SLEEP TIME

Listen to your intuition and trust you know what's best for yourself.

DINNER

SNACKS

EXERCISE / ACTIVITY

DAY 94

/ /

START WITH GRATITUDE

Today I am grateful about...

How I feel today:

PRIORITY GOALS

To love others you must first love yourself.

BREAKFAST

LUNCH

DINNER

SNACKS

WATER

SLEEP TIME

EXERCISE / ACTIVITY

When your cup is filled to the brim with love and acceptance of yourself, you are at peace with yourself. You are not in a constant need of approval, you don't project your issues onto others, you don't expect others to fill the void in your heart.

You can't pour from an empty cup. You need to love yourself first to be able to give love to others.

DAY 95

__/__/__

How I feel today:

○ ☹ ○ 😐 ○ ☺

START WITH GRATITUDE

Today I am grateful about...

PRIORITY GOALS

Self-love is the opposite of selfishness and narcissism.

WATER

SLEEP TIME

BREAKFAST

LUNCH

DINNER

SNACKS

EXERCISE / ACTIVITY

Never be afraid to love yourself because it might be seen as selfish or narcissistic by uneducated people.

» ***Narcissism***
is believing that you are better than everyone else, that everyone should respect you no matter what, that you are perfect.

» ***Self-love***
is believing that you are equal to everyone else, that you deserve respect just as everyone else, that you have flaws but so does every other human being.

What's one thing you can do today to make yourself FEEL CONTENT?

DAY 96

___/___/___

How I feel today:

○ ☹ ○ 😐 ○ ☺

START WITH GRATITUDE

Today I am grateful about...

PRIORITY GOALS

You cannot win your future if you cannot forgive your past.

– IKECHUKWU JOSEPH

At some point you just have to ***let go*** *of what you thought should or should not happen and* ***live*** *in what is happening.*

BREAKFAST

LUNCH

DINNER

SNACKS

WATER

SLEEP TIME

EXERCISE / ACTIVITY

Think of a negative event in your past. How can you use it as an OPPORTUNITY TO GROW?

DAY 97

__/__/__

How I feel today:

○ ☹ ○ 😐 ○ ☺

START WITH GRATITUDE

Today I am grateful about...

PRIORITY GOALS

You cannot travel back in time to fix your mistakes, but you can learn from them and forgive yourself for not knowing better.

– LEON BROWN

WATER

SLEEP TIME

BREAKFAST

LUNCH

DINNER

SNACKS

EXERCISE / ACTIVITY

Forgive yourself for what you have done and what you think you should have done or not. One bad deed does not make a good person bad. Just like one good act does not redeem the previous bad actions. At every moment you have had your reasons for the actions and decisions you have taken.

It's only human to
MAKE MISTAKES!
Remember a time when you could have used this reminder.

DAY 98

/ /

How I feel today:

START WITH GRATITUDE

Today I am grateful about...

PRIORITY GOALS

Happiness is when what you think, what you say, and what you do are in harmony.

– MAHATMA GANDHI

BREAKFAST

LUNCH

Reflect on this idea, and how closely aligned your actions, words, and thoughts are.

DINNER

SNACKS

EXERCISE / ACTIVITY

WATER

SLEEP TIME

DAY 99

/ /

How I feel today:

START WITH GRATITUDE

Today I am grateful about...

PRIORITY GOALS

You don't need to be perfect. Just be better than yesterday.

WATER

BREAKFAST

LUNCH

SLEEP TIME

What
3 QUESTIONS
would you want to ask an older version of yourself?

DINNER

SNACKS

What
3 THINGS WOULD YOU SHARE
with your 16-year-old self?

EXERCISE / ACTIVITY

DAY 100

___/___/___

How I feel today:

START WITH GRATITUDE

Today I am grateful about...

PRIORITY GOALS

Change is hard at first, messy in the middle and gorgeous at the end.

- ROBIN S. SHARMA

BREAKFAST

LUNCH

WATER

SLEEP TIME

DINNER

SNACKS

Congratulations, gorgeous! You made it to day 100.

EXERCISE / ACTIVITY

Thank yourself for the efforts, because it hasn't been easy.

Thank yourself for the mistakes, because you learn from them.

Thank yourself for wanting to be better.

100-DAY REFLECTION

THE BEST OF YOU

This is not the end, neither the beginning, but a going on.
100 steps out of countless more, each one leading to a better you.

Let this be your pledge too:

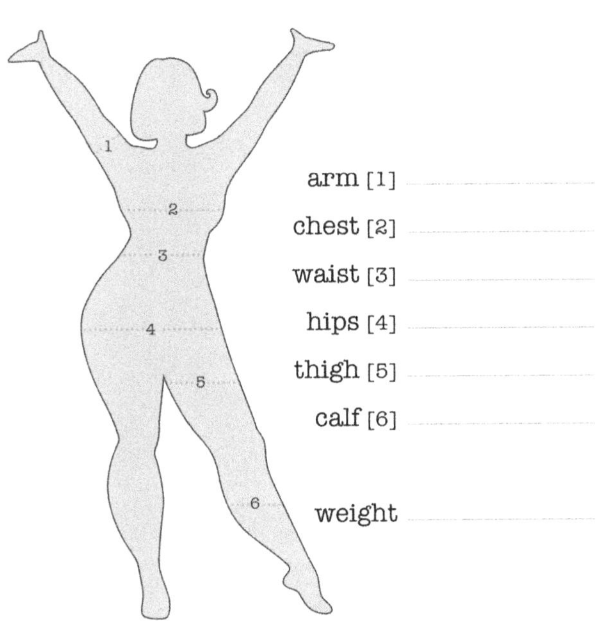

I am willing to be seen.
I am willing to speak up.
I am willing to keep going.
I am willing to listen
to what others have to say.
I am willing to go forward
even when I feel alone.
I am willing to go to bed each night,
at peace with myself.
I am willing to be my biggest,
best-est, most powerful self.

– EMMA WATSON

THINGS TO CONTINUE DOING:

THINK OF 3 GOOD THINGS THAT HAPPENED DURING THIS JOURNEY:

Hey gorgeous!

We are Happiness Creators. We have a passion for creating books that can improve and add joy to people's lives. Hopefully this journal will accomplish just that for you.

Self-care is giving the world the best of you instead of what's left of you.

– KATIE REED

HELP US MAKE OUR JOURNAL BETTER.

Tell us, which one was your favorite page?
Which one you disliked?
What would you like to change or add?
We'd love to hear from you, even if it is just to say hi.

And there is nothing more gratifying to us and putting more meaning to our work than hearing that our books have helped you.

Contact us at: **hello@happinesscreators.com**

And please, ***leave a review****, it really helps us!*

Take care and have a beautiful day,

Happiness Creators

Made in the USA
Las Vegas, NV
02 March 2024

86602285R00070